This book is dedicated to my children - Mikey, Kobe, and Jojo.

Copyright © 2024 Grow Grit Press LLC. All rights reserved. No part of this book may be reproduced in any form without permission in writing from the publisher. Please send bulk order requests to info@ninjalifehacks.tv

Paperback ISBN: 979-8-89614-039-9
Hardcover ISBN: 979-8-89614-041-2
eBook ISBN: 979-8-89614-040-5

Printed and bound in the USA.
NinjaLifeHacks.tv

Ninja Life Hacks®
by Mary Nhin

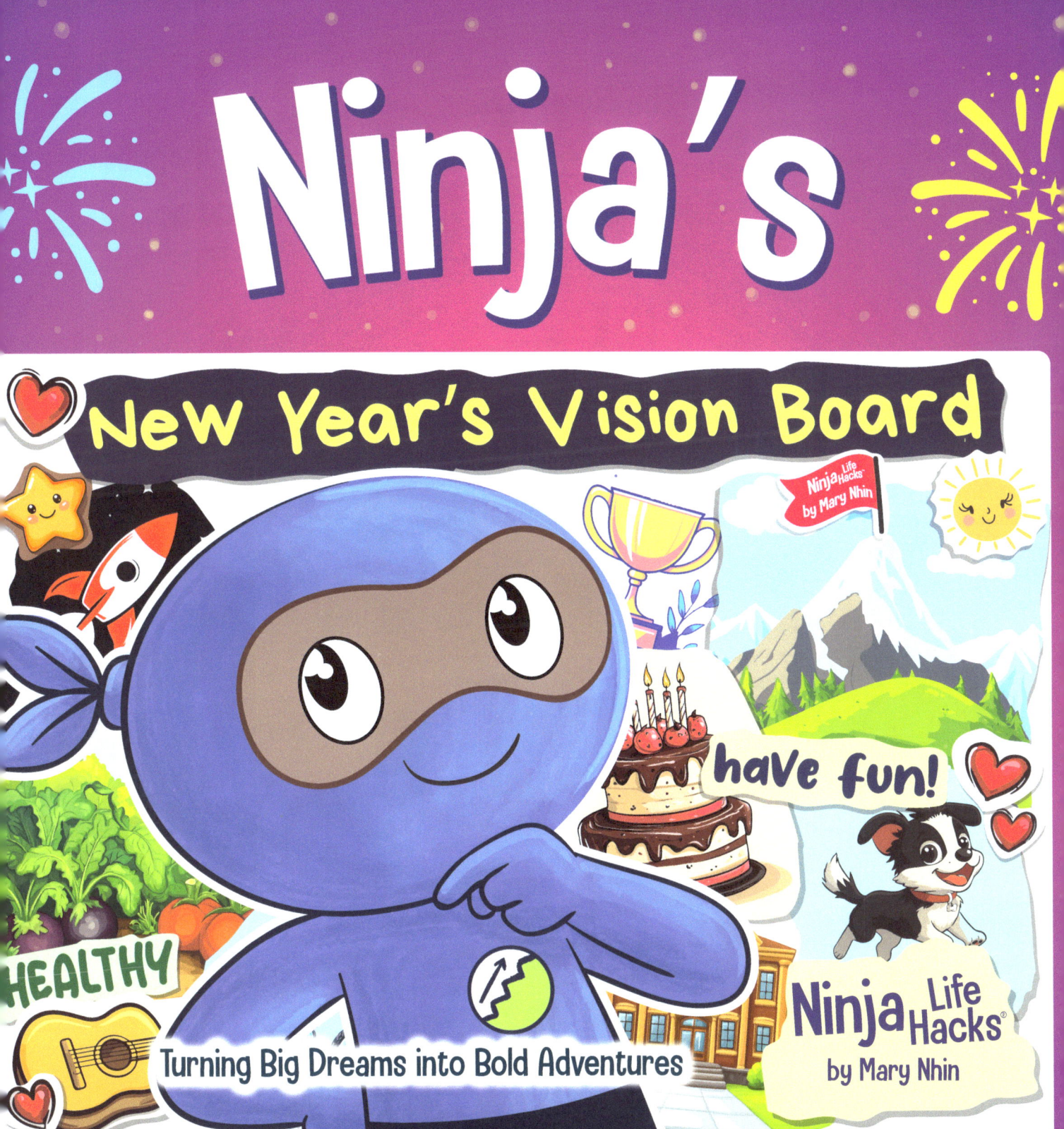

"But how do I focus? There's so much to do!" Ambitious groaned, pacing the floor.
"Create a vision board," Motivated replied.
"It will be a map to explore."

Ambitious gathered magazines, glue, and some pens,
She got crafty, cutting and pasting.
Pictures and words of the dreams she had
Were reminders that were long-lasting.

Ambitious hung her board up high on the wall
Where it glimmered in morning's light.
It was a mix of big dreams and small daily steps
Where she worked with all of her might.

Now every New Year, Ambitious starts with a plan,
Making vision boards to spark inspiration.
For the best way to reach the dreams in your heart,
Is with high hopes and a bit of creation.

Create Your Own Vision Board

What You'll Need:
- Magazines, newspapers, or printable images
- Glue sticks or tape
- Scissors
- A poster board or large sheet of paper
- Markers, crayons, or stickers

Instructions:
- Cut out pictures and words that represent your goals and dreams for the new year.
- Arrange them on your board to create a collage.
- Add drawings or decorations to make it unique.
- Hang your vision board somewhere you can see it every day!

Check out the fun Ninja's New Year's Vision Board lesson plans at ninjalifehacks.tv

I love to hear from my readers. Email me your feedback or thoughts on what my next story should be at info@ninjalifehacks.tv   Yours truly, Mary

 @marynhin   @GrowGrit
#NinjaLifeHacks

 Mary Nhin   Ninja Life Hacks

 Ninja Life Hacks

 @officialninjalifehacks

www.ingramcontent.com/pod-product-compliance
Lightning Source LLC
LaVergne TN
LVHW070436070526
838199LV00015B/521